PENGUIN PUZZLE TIME

Let's Play Tag!

⭐ Game

🔁 Repeat

⬛ Stop

INTERNET CONNECTION REQUIRED FOR AUDIO DOWNLOAD.

To use this book with the Tag™ Reader you must download audio from the LeapFrog® Connect Application.
The LeapFrog Connect Application can be downloaded and installed at leapfrog.com/connect.

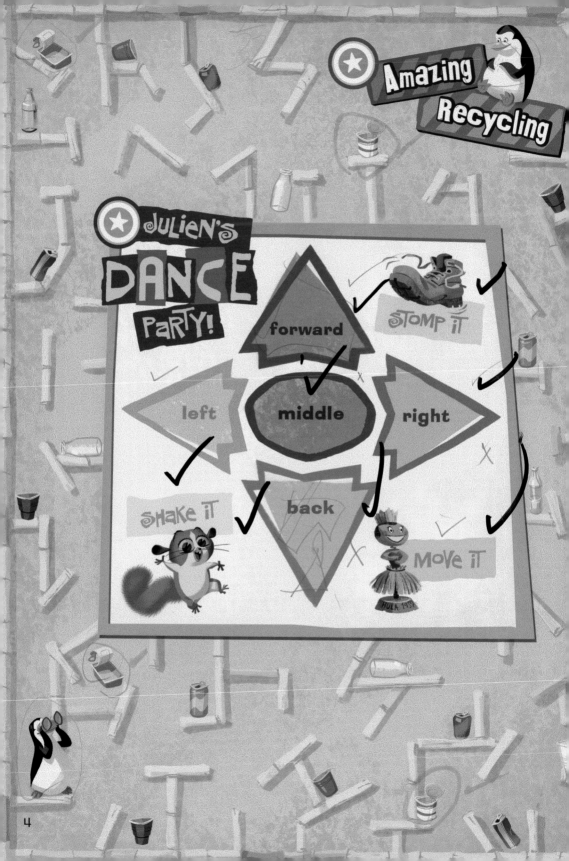

5

Lemurific Rhythms

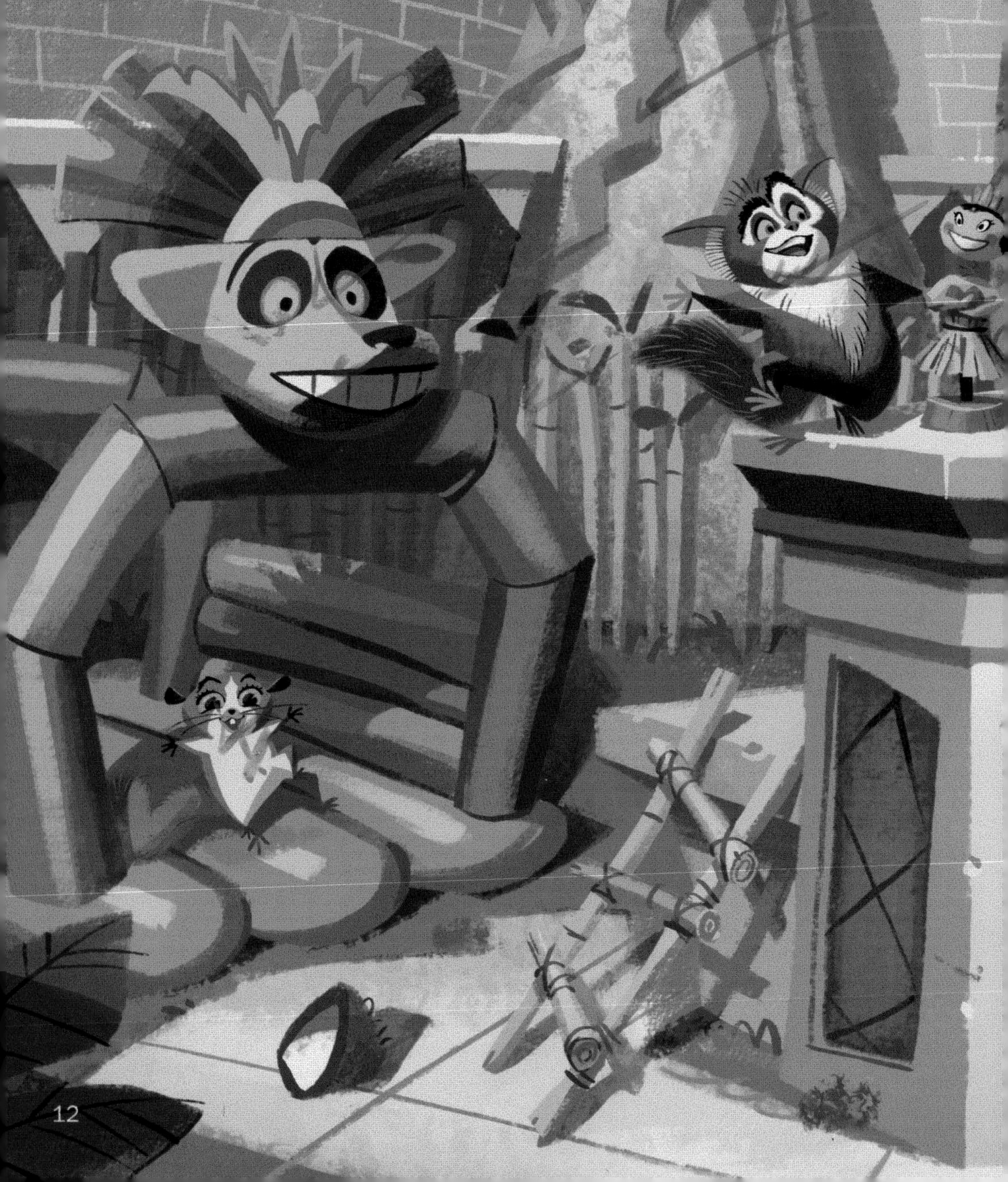

SEARCH AND SHOP

```
L F R K J G I A P E P O R S
A E C U B S Z N J I V M E U
N B M I L Q P P E N G U I N
Z A E U G Y L O G V A B W I
O L P Z R T R N F S C R N R
L L A L B Z C X M I A U H I
I P E T Z A O C B F T J R P
Z I O B G X T O E F I S H Q
```

APE	CUB	PET
BALL	FISH	SUN
CAT	LOG	ZOO

14

SHOPPING ☆ SAFARI

CALENDAR

Tropical
THURSDAY

Feeding
FRIDAY

Safari
SATURDAY

VISIT
to the
ZOO

Build a Tag™ library

Interactive Maps

Go on a geography journey
with your Tag™ Reader

*U.S. and World maps available Fall 2010

ou'll love!

Choose from more than 40 books and games*

The World of Cars

DORA the EXPLORER

GO DIEGO GO!

Learn to Read

Explore short and long vowels in two 6-book sets

Game Books

Explore skills beyond reading

I SPY

Green Eggs and Ham

By Dr. Seuss

Fancy NANCY